SimplyDog. Life lessons that bark.

By
Maria Peevey &
Megan Weinerman

Photographs by Megan Weinerman

SimplyShe™

Stewart, Tabori & Chang
New York

Maria's Note:
To my sister, follow your bliss because it's your life to live. To my niece Megan, remember you
can be anything you want to be, including a veterinarian. And to my nephews John and Ben,
dream extra big and don't let anyone or anything keep you from trying new things.

Conceived and created by SimplyShe™
copyright ©2003 by SimplyShe, Inc.

Published by Stewart, Tabori & Chang
A Company of La Martinière Groupe
115 West 18th Street
New York, NY 10011

Export Sales to all countries except Canada, France, and French-speaking Switzerland:
Thames & Hudson Ltrd.
181A High Holborn
London WC1V 7QX
England

Canadian Distribution:
Canadian Manda Group
One Atlantic Avenue, Suite 105
Toronto, Ontario M6K 3E7
Canada

ISBN: 1-58479-270-1

Printed in China

10 9 8 7 6 5 4 3 2 1

Sometimes it's just easier
to hear about enlightenment
from a dog.

Special thanks to all the animals and people who make my life fun. With particular thanks to Diane and Alex my favorite doggie sitters. Thanks too to my friends at Perfect Paws where I spend a lot of time playing, and to everyone else who loves me.
– Reh

At an early age, Reh [that's "her" spelled backwards] realized that she had an important gift to give. That gift is her perspective on life. It doesn't hurt that Reh also has the kind of star quality that other dogs only dream about and people want to be near. Frankly, she is more fun to hang out with than most people. And she is often better looking.

"If you think you're great, then you probably are."

– Reh

1. Reh has charisma. People smile and stare when she walks down the street. It gives her a great feeling knowing she makes others happy just by being herself.

[the bark] Whatever you do, make it look good.

2. Reh lives in a nice neighborhood. She has a pretty yard, a soft bed and great toys. While others may be dissatisfied with what they have, Reh doesn't believe the grass is greener on the other side. She's pretty good at keeping things green on her side.

[the bark] Want what you have.

3. Reh is confident that her perception of reality is right on target. And she especially feels that being shorter than everyone else gives her this advantage.
[the bark] An enlightened viewpoint depends on where you're standing.

4. Reh fell in love but she had to end it. She knew they were just too different to make it work. Love is like a tennis ball, she thought. Sometimes you find what you're looking for and sometimes it just isn't worth the effort of bringing it back. [the bark] Relationships are tough.

5. Reh is proud of her nose. She thinks it's her best feature. People tell her it's big and uneven in skin tone compared to the rest of her face. But she doesn't care. In fact, whenever someone takes her picture, she always insists on a close-up. [the bark] Work with what you've got.

6. Reh gets a kick out of making new friends. Sometimes, to entertain herself, she sits perfectly still and waits for the other person to check if she's breathing. This proves to be quite an introduction.

[the bark] It's up to you to make it happen.

7. Christmas hung over Reh's head like a cheap Santa hat. She was bloated from holiday parties, had no time to shop, and considered it a stressful time of year. But then she remembered, "Wait a minute. I'm a dog!" Then she felt better. [the bark] When overwhelmed, seek perspective.

8. Reh is a backseat driver. Which has something to do with the fact that she always sits in the back seat and can't drive. But boy, does she know how to give directions without being asked. [the bark] Keep it to yourself.

9. Reh hates to beg, especially where food is concerned. She feels it's demeaning. But she's also practical. She knows that sometimes you have to compromise to get what you want. [the bark] If you end up at the right place who cares how you got there.

10. Reh found herself in a hole. She wasn't quite sure what to do about it but she accepted the situation for what it was—an opportunity to dig deep. [the bark]
A hole is what you make it.

11. Whenever life gets Reh down, she searches for what's making her sad, and takes steps to change it. Then she goes shopping. [the bark] Happiness is a process.

12. Reh had a rough day at the office, so when she got home she started gnawing on her old stuffed bear to unwind. She knew it was a disgusting habit, but she figured that since she had kicked the booze and cigarettes, she was allowed this one last vice.

[the bark] Perfection is overrated.

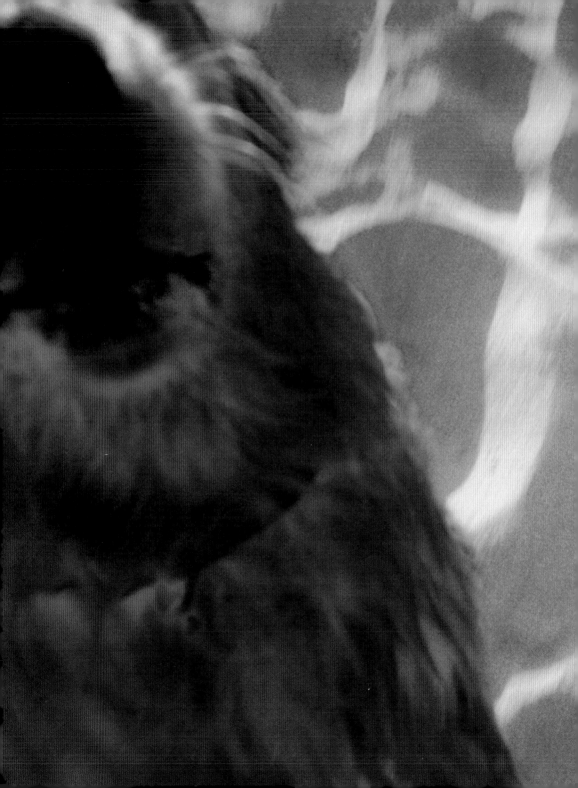

13. Reh enjoys her time alone. She's tired of hearing people complain about her daring habit of eating unidentifiable things off the ground. After all, it isn't her problem if they can't understand the thrill of the unknown. [the bark] Freedom comes when you stop caring what others think.

14. Reh's daily mantra consists of saying "yes" to life. This means she has a hard time envisioning "no." At least this is the excuse she uses when she does things she isn't supposed to do. [the bark] There are many kinds of truth.

15. Reh refuses to be manipulated. She ignores those who try to con her to get what they want. She's much smarter than that. She knows that nothing is free in life, especially dog snacks. [the bark] Some treats aren't worth the price.

At an early age, Reh knew she was destined for something great. Although others seemed content with their lives, she wanted more. And that "more" included hiring someone to fetch the ball for her so she would never have to do it again. [the bark] Dream big.

17. Reh likes acting. It gives her a chance to experiment with different personalities. Since she's comfortable with herself, she's never afraid of pretending to be something she isn't. [the bark] Imagine what could be.

18. Reh believes persistence seasoned with subtlety is the key to accomplishing a goal. With this winning tactic she can taste all that the future has in store. [the bark] Don't give up.

19. Reh tried to be patient, but she couldn't believe her friends were late again. She hated to wait. This was exactly why she herself was never on time. [the bark] You get back what you give.

20. An overwhelming sense of emptiness rippled through Reh's being. She began to question her existence. For a brief moment, her life seemed so . . . meaningless. But then her stomach growled and she realized she was just hungry. [the bark] When in doubt, eat.

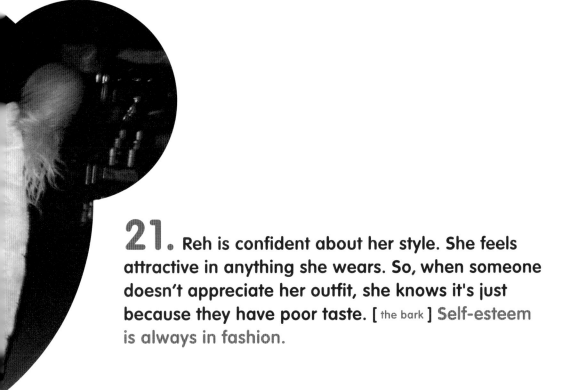

21. Reh is confident about her style. She feels attractive in anything she wears. So, when someone doesn't appreciate her outfit, she knows it's just because they have poor taste. [the bark] Self-esteem is always in fashion.

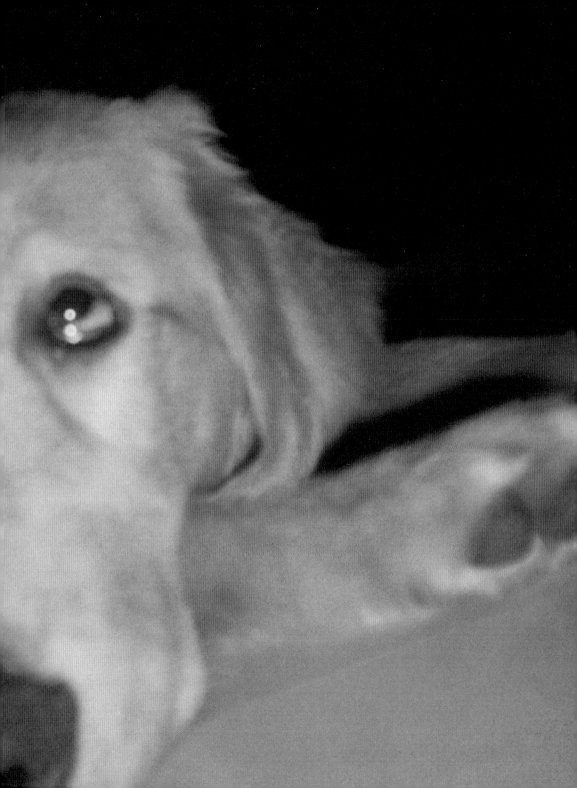

22. Reh understands that the basis of a healthy relationship is open communication and active listening. But she finds that most people only like the talking part.

[the bark] If it sounds like a monologue, it probably is.

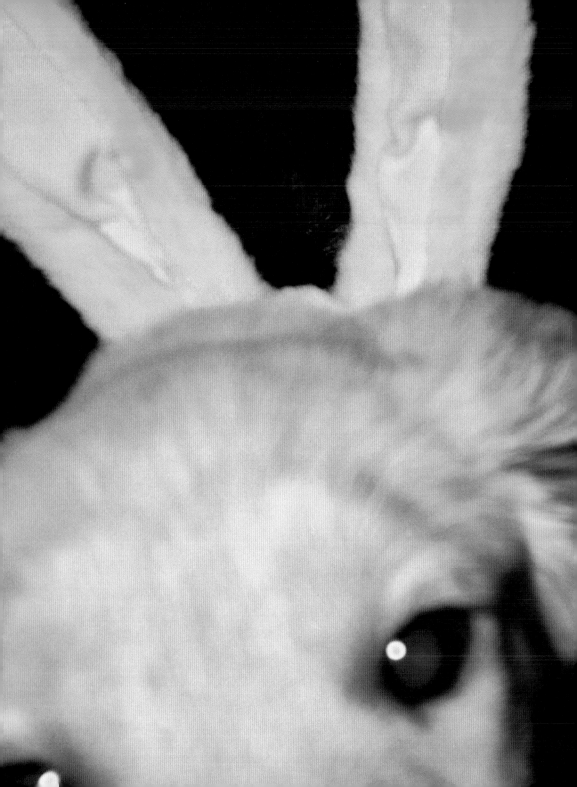

23. Reh is good at playing make-believe. But dressing up as the Easter Bunny has its disadvantages. Frankly, dyeing eggs and wearing big ears is exhausting. But if it gives people what they want, who is she to complain? [the bark] Everyone needs something to believe in.

24. Reh has a great sense of humor. This comes in handy when she's surrounded by others who take themselves too seriously. She feels sorry for them, but recognizes that not everyone knows how to amuse herself in tight situations. [the bark] There's always a place for laughter even if you're the only one laughing.

25. Reh was single again. She knew starting over would not be easy. It terrified her to think of going it alone. But she also wanted to believe that all things happen for a reason. That explanation seemed a tad convenient but it was all she had to work with. [the bark]

Don't let fear keep you from going where you need to go.

26. Reh knows how to relax and have fun. And she doesn't let anyone make her feel guilty about it. She believes others are simply too addicted to stress. Clearly, she still has much to teach. [the bark] Enjoy your life.

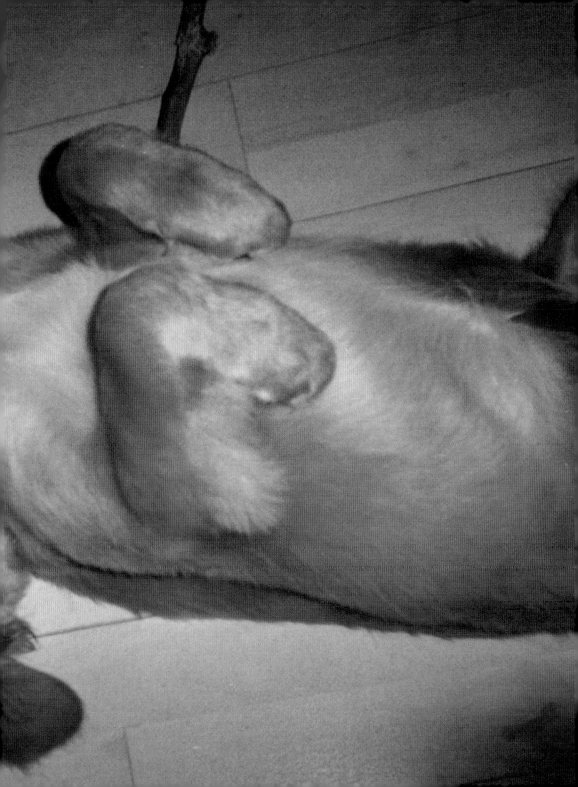

27. Reh took a moment for self-reflection. She was grateful for her loving family. She was proud of her relationships with her friends. And she was particularly impressed with how great her hair looked—wet or dry.

[the bark] Not everything has a point.

[barking points]

[1]
Whatever you do, make it look good.

[2]
Want what you have.

[3]
An enlightened viewpoint depends on
where you're standing.

[4]
Relationships are tough.

[5]
Work with what you've got.

[6]
It's up to you to make it happen.

[7]
When overwhelmed, seek perspective.

[8]
Keep it to yourself.

[9]
If you end up at the right place who cares
how you got there.

[10]
A hole is what you make it.

[11]
Happiness is a process.

[12]
Perfection is overrated.

[13]
Freedom comes when you stop caring what others think.

[14]
There are many kinds of truth.

[15]
Some treats aren't worth the price.

[16]
Dream big.

[17]
Imagine what could be.

[18]
Don't give up.

[19]
You get back what you give.

[20]
When in doubt, eat.

[21]
Self-esteem is always in fashion.

[22]
If it sounds like a monologue, it probably is.

[23]
Everyone needs something to believe in.

[24]
There's always a place for laughter
even if you're the only one laughing.

[25]
Don't let fear keep you from going where you need to go.

[26]
Enjoy your life.

[27]
Not everything has a point.

About the Authors

Maria and Megan live and work in San Francisco. They started a company called SimplyShe. They laugh a lot. Reh is Maria's dog even though Maria sometimes thinks Reh likes Megan better. But that's because Megan bribes her with snacks and back rubs.

Also by Maria Peevey and Megan Weinerman
Are You My Boyfriend?
I Love My Hair!

Ramon Estrada / Los Angeles

Maria Peevey and Megan Weinerman